Two Minds

Two Minds

Harold Rhenisch

 **Frontenac House Poetry**

Book design: Neil Petrunia, Epix Design
Cover Image: Harold Rhenisch
Author photo: George Kusyj

Library and Archives Canada Cataloguing in Publication

Rhenisch, Harold, 1958-, author
        Two minds / Harold Rhenisch.

Poems.
"Quartet 2015".
Issued in print and electronic format.
ISBN 978-1-927823-36-1 (pbk.).–ISBN 978-1-927823-37-8
(pdf).–ISBN 978-1-927823-38-5 (html)

        I. Title.

PS8585.H54T86 2015   C811'.54   C2015-903335-7
                                                C2015-903336-5

Frontenac House gratefully acknowledges the support of the Canada Council for the Arts for our
publishing program. We would also like to thank the Government of Alberta Multimedia Development
Fund for their support of our publishing program.

Canada Council   **Conseil des Arts**
for the Arts   **du Canada**   *Alberta* Government

Printed and bound in Canada
Published by Frontenac House Ltd.
1138 Frontenac Ave. SW
Calgary, Alberta, T2T 1B6, Canada
Tel: 403-245-8588

Contents

The Man With the Head of a Stag Speaks

Outside the forest of words,
outside the protection of knowledge, all deer have a human shape.

Swallowed water trickles for months, moss-cool,
down through fluted bones.

Goddesses of charred iron fashion themselves by building cairns
on a blue glacial plain in winter,

adding stones year by year as they pass,
until the shapes take on human forms,

each with its back to the sun
and staring into the motionless black centre of the sky.

Everything and Nothing

To see into the mind, look to the farthest distance;
it is not given form in the world.

The philosophers who paced through their moonlit gardens
did not attempt to join what is already one.

The whole world and all of time can be seen,
even by the smallest child, even in a rufus hummingbird,

hanging, bronze, on the tip of a spring willow —
once only, and again once only, and again. Only once.

The Return to the Trees

The birds have replaced their feathers with larkspur petals.
All night the pounding of hooves thunders through small rocks.

Cold determines nothing.
Nothing determines the cold.

The wind catches the petals of the cornflowers on the gravel shoulder,
then sweeps over the road: conch shells.

Memory is my country held to the air.
As I forget it with each passing year, it weighs on me more heavily.

It has taken my first forty years to come to this:
red ants scurry over the horses' flanks

as if a school of trout, muscular and cold,
were slipping through the trunks of birches and over my gloved hands.

For Children's Eyes Only

Within the loon the cry.
Within the leaf the swell breaking on shingle.

The blue of the mountain goat climbing above the scree:
trembling fingers reaching under water,

the mathematics of a wave retreating from breaking.
The hills have drowned in grass.

I walk out into the mountain dawn.
The mountains walk in.

Within the stone, the shadow.
Within the shadow, the shadow.

After the End of the Summer but Before Summer Has Ended

What is not to be understood: the apple beating in the chest.
Rain: a tomato sprinkled with salt and eaten standing up.

The high edge of the call of a bittern in moonlight:
within the lesson, the word speaking speaking.

A scattering of mica on gravel: inside the fire the stone,
the sun learning to tie the sutures of water.

All that is known once only and known deeply:
pursed lips lapping with the touch of a mind.

The Shell Game

The shadow that casts a path of darkness:
the frog pulsing within the scales of a cedar.

A lintel knows even its own absence.
Millstones arrive in circles, until they crack.

Is, what always was, always is.
What can be mapped can be followed.

The eyes of a dog on the trail of a pheasant: an eddy.
A bear is a violin.

At dawn, grass walks into the distance and takes on
the cool of the cheek. Iron knows only verbs.

Within the tension of wood, the flicker.
Within the flicker, the flex of wood.

A child calls out of distance, her hands full of walnuts:
the earth rising in fire, shedding all but naked presence.

The repeat of a wave: how to sing a stone in a minor key.
The mind in its shell, thinking: the shell in its mind.

Plan of the Ideal Library,
Designed for Home Construction

Preferably it will be built out-of-doors.
Is there any possible way you can get hold of some brook trout?

A blacksmith's shop would be a good setting,
the wind and the mosquitoes streaming in the window — that can't be shut.

Maybe someone smashing a hammer down on an anvil
now and again — to keep you awake.

You could even hire someone to work that part — like Parks Canada!
Water would be fun — and some old air,

stuff from 1890 or something,
without any Vancouver in it.

You could just release it there — as a blessing.
Cook's Dry American Champagne:

Warning: Do Not Point this Bottle
Anywhere Near Your Face.

The Weight of the World

The winter lives within the wings of a rooster.
Horses dream of apples and curraghs.

An ant walks across the red coals of a fire.
Nothing watches nothing.

Women walk to and fro among the flames with water in their hands.
The language of love is a wafer of melon on a crystal plate.

A match burns within the idea of a thought within the body of an eye.
Every true book is bound with pages of beaten iron.

Rain: the sudden cold of the stratosphere on the cheek.
Wind: a piece of cloth caught in a door.

Who is the book and who is the reader?
Questions are not answers. Answers are questions.

A window flies through the sky on the wings of a hawk.
Vast cathedrals of stone rise up, full of nesting birds.

Water is a cat's cradle,
but the world has no weight, at all.

The Weight of the Sky Over a Shaman's Fire

We are to speak of that which is not to be seen.
The thunder picks the house up and empties it.

Slow constellations turn around the pole.
The cage of my ribs is a drum.

Wise men are paid for their work with silence.
The cathedral is a machine for drowning.

The past rises up each stalk of bulrush until it is smoke.
I carry a bone rattle in my hands.

The weight of a raindrop is no longer instinctual.
Our voices are beings reconstructed as combines.

The old language is spoken solely by trees.
Only the absence of a bear is perceived.

Silence is meant to talk out loud like a dog barking.
The crow of a rooster is the cry of a child.

Our voices are columns of figures and matrices of symbols.
I have learned a new language, but to whom can I speak it?

A white horse walks up to me from the trees.
I knock an apple from a high branch.

The horse pulls back its black lips and eats. For a moment
I am all fingers, then I am an open hand.

Night, After Months of Cloud

Plato wrote that there is the idea of a tree.
My memories are folded silk handkerchiefs.

Every day words come to me from a greater distance. Hello, Rußland.
Fields reflect the sky. What does the sky reflect?

Memory is a city of rusted iron rivets in the body of a bluebird.
A bluebird is an aircraft made of discarded whalebone corsets.

My guidance system is a white stone angel,
but the body of a horse stands still for hours, around its bones.

Ribcages run along the edge of the trees, say the gravediggers,
in the language of trees.

The world is a hymn sung by a cricket under a granite wall.
Barbed wire exists to be carried into the Alps by partisans.

A lone walker treks six months north on a plain of tongues.
The city library falls onto the trees of the high plateau as rain.

The whales have swallowed the stars. It's that simple.
They sparkle like vast zeppelins floating in. They are that far.

They strain the cities out through their baleen:
caribou, carrying the first snow in their mouths. They are that close.

A Recipe for Bread and Wine

On one side of the city there is sound. On the other,
Rosa Luxembourg explains the hermeneutics of canals.

The world vanishes between each breath;
day by day the sun is becoming a forest.

The bodies of men are thin seed pods burning with starlight.
Death is an intricate story of the birth of presence.

I speak to carry the body beyond the arm's tuck and turn.
Tonight we will walk through the flames. And in the morning.

Don't look away. Don't look for easier passage.
The sun falls to earth yet the earth rises into the sun.

Exodus From the Land of the Dead

The dead walk among us. And where do we walk?
Within the sparrow: the twig. Within the twig, the wind.

Columns of refugees push through the trees. Endlessly.
The city of the past is on fire. We are matches.

The ancestors are choking. Starved and confused,
they stumble into ranch yards. Grandmothers glare.

Iamblichus said that god is present in stone truly carved.
The hands of lovers grip each other and then release,

release each other and then grip,
grip each other and then don't let go.

Love Song in Middle Age

The white swans have returned to swamps of black water.
There are physical dimensions to thought. You are one.

It takes such a large body to harness the quick tongue;
I am pulling thistles while geese fly south over bare hills.

You can choose to destroy the earth. You can preserve it.
In the desert of snow, a king's crown blinds thought's fool.

A city springs up in each of a shaman's paths: snow.
The stars are not seen. They are known. They are followed.

Crows that fly through the space between water and cloud open.
A deer sees both snow and falling rain at once, at once.

The wind is not blowing. The snow is not falling.
You are. I am. And we?

To escape the binding charms of words, pick up a stone.
Hold it. Be held. Hold. Be.

Autumn Moon, After Reading

Armies know this as quickly as this knows armies:
there is only one war; there are endless forms of peace.

Priests sit in the temple squares as they collect the sun;
the wind tears the temples away, leaving the priests in cubes of light.

A red horse climbs the ladder of a blue field,
its head bowed, pulling a heavy weight. This is our task as well.

Because books are emigrating closer and closer to an approximation of sound,
I have left my books on my desk and have gone out to the birds.

There is frost on the air. A single blue wind is striking the whole coast at once.
A man I was walks through the furrows, with stalks of wheat for hair.

His hands are sparrows that splash off on a cold current of wind.
Their shadows move together over the broken soil. This way, that way.

The man has a wasp nest for a head. This way.
He lifts it off and pushes it up into the sky. That way. It floats.

Blowing out Matches at Eleusis

The sky has permeated the soil. Wherever we are,
we walk on the songs of crickets — whoever we are.

When I have been a window, I have been a bird.
I have held a lake in my mouth, while it was flying.

The sun burns in the breast of each sparrow;
in each sparrow the same sun.

As to why swallows have not invented speech,
well, things are their names;

because the grass lives in silence,
it amplifies sound and sends it on.

I have built a house of field stones that remember the sea.
Every year the plow turns them over one by one to face the stars.

Plato opened a doorway into the earth. He found potatoes.
The earth walked through it into the light, and was gone.

Harvest Song for Washboard and Cricket

For weeks, the aspens have been torn out of yellow silk
curtains before a window of flowing water.

I've picked up books, I've tasted soil, I've smelled
the cold in damp leaves. My hands are burlap sacks.

The sun quickly leafs through the chapter on Kierkegaard
to the chapter on the aluminum alloy construction of aircraft frames.

Then it goes dark. All summer, swallows cast shadows
that moved the length and height of the room, and over us.

A blackbird hangs upside down from a sunflower poised over the soil.
There are old libraries in which such books are shelved. It is dark there.

Yellow ripples of light float over our hands and faces,
as we stare up at the birds, right here, our gills opening and closing, right now.

The process of emptiness leads from conception to trial.
Sleep needs the mind. It burns it into dust. Cough, Cough.

I have a wooden bowl carved by my grandfather. I carry away the past in my hands
and scatter it to the winds. The winds lift it, up.

I am on a long journey to a city of sparrows and amaranth.
Stars spin slowly through the rooms, in immense height.

I catch a bird in my hand. The bird speaks me with its wings.
I catch myself in my mind. I open my hands and set myself free.

Words are a drug sipped out of leather sacks while picking rocks.
In our absence, all the proof we need, the world endures.

Instructions for the Winter Ceremony

When a grain of wheat falls on the soil, a blackbird rises up.
In Hamlet's century, everything seemed and nothing was.

Some drops of rain never land. I can't stand within my body anymore;
that bungalow has gone up in flame.

Each of the thousand leaves of an aspen sapling
turns the same way to face the light, then releases its yes.

When listening to the sky trumpetting for snow
the choice is not to walk back to a stutter of sparrows.

10,000 years ago, a shaman tracked deep into the night.
Now he is coming back. I meet him at the door. I open.

You Are in the Forest Between
Czernowitz and Prague

The sun has hunkered down into the trees rimming the earth.
I speak with the rusted voice of a grouse in golden grass.

Death wears tall leather books and purrs. You, too,
come from a story told in a forest as dark as boot black.

Snow falls. Armies clank by in the night.
I scatter lumps of bread in old snow.

Every Roman had a puppet in his eye.
Freud sits in his study in Vienna and tamps his pipe: tap tap.

We are coming to the cities, bearing elixirs.
Each night we smash the neck off one. One.

Breath is a divination.
After a long journey, we return home with glass for the windows.

On his deathbed, Baudelaire revised the critique of pure reason.
A young poet's fingers smell of cordite. It washes off.

Everyone in the Script Is Macbeth

A soldier calls to the faces of days that have long left him.
The white flashes of leaves turn over in the wind.

Wolves circle in the heart's pool, with iron teeth.
I stand between dawn and dusk, painted blue.

Crows fly through vast skies of eggshell.
Trees are rooting in my feet; there is no longer a king.

I no longer remember the message I set out with those years ago.
Horsemen are thundering across the plains in snow.

Drink the black trees. We are not on a journey.
The entire sky is descending on beating wings.

The tracks of the wolves fill in.
Then they vanish.

Contract for the Transport of a Piano

Snow is weaving the mantle of the world.
I am a window's workings working loose.

A woman walks through summer rain, plucking roses.
She is the answer to a question she hasn't posed.

What do the words dream of when we are not there
to dream of our words? Hands?

Hush, here we are. Here we are, Hush.
We are hush here. Hush, we are, here.

Socrates Wears a Black Collar with Silver Spikes

Death is always employed by life. There has been confusion.
I am walking through storm. The storm barks.

I scatter lumps of bread in the snow that birds eat at dawn.
Take the hand I offer. This forest belongs to the trees.

The snow lies thick underfoot.
The sun is falling into the colour of high oxygen.

No-one can take your name from you.
Say it over and over to me. You. You. You.

Petals Drift Upon the Stones of a Mountain River

Cold air slips down among the roots of the grasses.
Two bodies tangled in a bed kick off linen,

lip to breast to fingers running down the spine.
These are the lonely moors of ancient song.

Early in the morning, it is enough to say the body moves
with the moving body then evaporates.

Plato heard women's voices singing among stones —
and wrote them down, so now it's still there,

the cicadas still sing, the heat of the stones
is here. No more water can be added to the cup

that is dipped into the river, no water
can be poured out.

As the Riverbed Forms Itself Into a Trout, It Swallows the Sky

In the long hollow chambers of my bones,
the sweet wheat grass drums beneath the skies.

Snow that falls within April light is evening
drawn out on a violin made of caught breath.

Hounds run endlessly over snow, running down game.
I am the game. I hide in a thicket, dappled with sun.

Rain falls as green as a river over my uplifted face;
milkweed flowers out of my fingernails. I live for the hunt.

The grouse I am, the beat of the drum, my weeping name:
the ash within the fire swallowing the swallow in the flame.

All Fall Down

The world that is the world begins
with the ladder of integration, which has no rungs.

The fingers climb the violin as the violin
climbs the mind watching snow fall before a window.

Before the mind watches, the window is demure lace
traced with trees and horses clopping through memory.

After the mind, the city applauds with white doves
set free in hands clasped and unclasped.

Above the eelskin river the cathedral,
above the cathedral the wind,

above the wind — and now there is laughter,
because there is nothing above the wind.

East of the West

The moon is a limpet. The herons come out
long after the blackberries have become thorns.

This is the land of salt. Crows celebrate light.
They keep it. Men drop nets.

I walk past a seal rising out of the kelp.
An iron bed has washed up on the sand, among clams.

Herakleitos said you can only stand in a river once.
This shore is where rivers wait for us.

The sun stretches from horizon to horizon.
It is a long time from now.

I can touch this stone. Look, I pick it up.
I drop it. Look, I pick up this one. I drop it.

Midsummer Moon Above the Nootka Fault

I am not the movement but the moment.
Jellyfish lie on the rocks like carnations.

No one picks the wild apples on this shore.
Wind blows through their six-inch thorns.

The waves knick logs around like bells.
Children come in the evenings and light fires.

Fire, water, salt, and air: crow talk,
heron song, those mad old Greeks.

Ebb and Flow

Mourners in parade are glassed with eyes half shut.
Gulls do the stitching.

In this season, loons are returning from the mountains.
Daughters of the rain coming to the cloud's cold grave.

Mystery: a tug pulling a mountain from the blue south.
Knowledge: a city floats down from the north. It is white.

When herons stand still enough, dogs do not see them.
I am above a fault line. I swim on foot.

A painter told me it is impossible to see a crow.
Today, absence is eating salmon eggs. We are all estuaries.

I told the painter that crows are stories crows tell.
Crows make cracks about pheasants.

I would say when I walk along this shore I walk through myself
at the speed that my self walks through me. I know better.

I pick a blackberry from among thorns. I brush
off wasps and pop the black sun into my mouth.

When I was young, I saw drowned men in the waves.
Now I see waves.

The City of the River That Tears Boulders to the Sea

Black clouds build over the continent.
We sail on drowned cliff faces.

Old men struggle down the shore to cut firewood.
It is a trick done with blue smoke and gumboots.

The moon tonight is the thinnest of crescents.
A black wolf chews my gloves. Even his claws are black.

A friend takes photographs of gates in a warehouse.
On each of them, Christ is a blooming Dionysus.

Another friend paints a warning sign for electrocution.
On the edge of a grey ocean, this counts as landscape.

There is a people with only one word for rain.
They live inside adjectives.

The bingo players have taken over from the Freemasons.
The film maker's union owns your TV set. Don't watch things get ugly.

I have watched men stand for an afternoon in a river,
with the water flowing around their thighs. They have light switches.

The oldest part of town has bars on its windows.
Everyone wants in, especially at night.

December is spring in this climate.
The mosses and the mallards dress in emerald light.

The scientists do not approve of this talk.
This talk is not for them.

The Power Plant

The falls are almost dry now. People
walk down a slippery trail to see the past, but they make it.

Where the rain has been turned into a reservoir,
the bodies we wake to are metaphors. What is a metaphor.

The last philosophers wrote the autobiography of economic man.
Then they took down their walls and left their foundations.

The flu clinic is held in the Catholic Church. We practice dying.
The parking lot has directional arrows, but no sidewalks.

At solstice, the sea and the air are the same colour.
We stop. The late sun shines from all of us at once. We stop again, then go on.

Conservation and Rebirth

One day, eagles are chasing each other through the trees.
The next day a man neglects to bury a dead horse.

The rain drums on the skylights of a deaf man's house.
Periodically, he goes to the door to see who wants to come in.

We have wrapped our banana trees in Salvation Army sheets.
At 11 a.m. all staff go to the back room to pray. The poor wait.

The First People are sitting on the grey rocks of the breakwater.
They have not forgotten we are remembering something that used to exist.

The mountains are being taken down and loaded on rusty ships.
At the next dock, rich women are painting their yachts. I go back and forth.

Luther said, "My God is an impenetrable fortress."
Bach set it to music. We buy it from amazon.de., on plastic.

Despite quantum mechanics, there is only one earth.
Although there is only one earth, there is quantum mechanics.

Look up. Along the river, pink salmon used to stink to high heaven.
Linguists are now hired to decipher the language of machines.

Salmon are now being raised in net pens.
Things are looking up. They're getting out.

Shutting Down the Pulp Mill

The smell of money is the smell of sulfur.
In the earliest dramas, the devil had all the best parts.

The river city players put on a show with twenty acting parts.
Most of the players aren't acting, so the audience does.

This is the only city in which a dead man writes a newspaper column.
A penned fish can be owned, until it gets out.

The town's leaders worship Mithras, who slaughtered the sun.
Marinated or not, the only bulls in town have already been cut into steaks.

At the farmer's market, the belly dancer brings her own ghetto blaster.
Termites fly over the August water and drown.

The first people here climbed out of the tide and took a deep breath.
The churches on this shore have spires, like masts.

When the wind is from the north, for fifty years
the air went up like a match. We are sweeping up the ash.

Waiting Out the Storm

A Dutch soprano sings a German prayer.
Her body is a reed that she allows the wind to fill. No, to flood.

A thousand years ago, geese overwintered on the moon.
They were halfway to Heaven. So were we.

Two weeks ago a Russian gull landed on the estuary.
The police ordered people to stay out of the snow.

There is no air above the ocean, but there are white clouds.
I shovel the sky to my door, then I stomp it off my boots and go in.

Putting Down Roots Gingerly

There is snow on the ground and rain on the windows.
I eat cookies glazed with lemon juice and sugar.

Honey bread is a prayer you knead with your hands.
If done right, it begins almost as a liquid. Then there are stars.

A rat has found the apples. She is feeding her babies.
Everything we own is packed in cardboard, then unpacked.

One tablespoon of yeast is enough to bring forth a god.
One god at a time is enough: the wisdom of hawthorns.

In this climate, holly grows as a weed.
So do blackberries. So do we.

Christmas Evensong

A man searches for himself through the pattern of his fingers.
The earliest home organs were powered by women dancing with ribbons.

Even in the afternoon, the service is just beginning.
I hear through ears made out of hair and the thinnest titanium.

My daughter complains she has never seen me without a beard.
I tell her that was another person — a harpsichord.

One electron excites another electron which excites
another electron which excites another. Life is a theorem, too.

In the deepest snow, drivers stop and put on chains.
Each snowflake lasts for a moment in the river, then it is the river.

Red-headed mergansers eddy through a spawning channel constructed by
bulldozer.
The fish don't come back anymore. We do.

I crouch in the dog's doorway and push straw in the corners.
The next morning, the poor baby smells like Bethlehem.

Remembering Paul Celan

What works for the fox doesn't always work for the hound-o.
The fattest goose is often the smallest when it is cooked.

All numbers greater than one are sometimes one.
Bookshelves are built to bear considerable weight.

When libraries were private, men invented science.
Now that they are public, they write historical novels.

Descartes wrote, I think therefore I am.
Modern mathematics was invented to cheat at dice games.

Einstein was a patent clerk. Much has been made of that
by people who've never owned a Swiss watch made of plastic.

The northern edge of an empire is still its heart,
the poet of the holocaust wrote in a foreign language.

An army marches on its stomach, but sleeps on its feet.
Sometimes a man is locked up for being of two minds. Sometimes he escapes.

Where They Were all Along

Cup the wind in the hands, sense it turn to rain: that is music.
I swallow the lake in one mouthful.

When I breathe out, the sudden white cloud of an apple
tree in bloom, sweetly-scented, billows in the air.

Slowly it dissipates in acid sunlight until only fish are left,
leaping through the surface of the sky to catch stars

caught on its drifting surface, then splashing down.
It is one world and one moment, burning and cool.

In the same way the trees along the shore
grow into themselves but do not see the light;

they drink it, burning with a fire
that predates the translation of thought into action.

We thought we were living among the stars,
but the stars have been living among us.

Open-Eyed One

Light through the window, the voice of Chopin: all things are fire.
What draws us together in the cold is not the cold.

In the forest, you will find men and women who used to live in houses.
The moon lies on the ground like a sheet smoothed down by hand.

The world is a crow walking on the bed of the river.
Long ago the painter became his painting. All this you know, but the words do not:

you are walking from the world's end to its beginning.
Bandits ride down into the valleys to plunder anyone not staying here forever.

In the spring people bang wooden clappers to wake themselves.
There is something that needs to be said, that only quiet can answer.

Come closer. The city of flowers and old books has vanished.
I dream of a field, in which a single white horse stands in rain. Now it grows dark.

Time is never the same for the one who speaks and the one who listens.
It is the same if I lose something or if I find it.

In the middle of my life, I return to old fields.
The crickets sing of the civilization of grasses. I practice being born.

The Surf at the Edge of the World

The streams are poured into small green bottles
and delivered around the world.

Convoys of trucks pass through the night.
In the mountains, the water no longer flows.

People climb slowly over silver stones
until they reach the cliffs. They lay

their faces on the hot stone
and sense the heaviness of the world.

They breathe it in. They breathe it out.
They breathe it out some more.

Wherever You Are You Know You Are There

In the water the sun is a green leaf.
In the air it is a candle.

Nights, on the edge of a plain of ghosts and ashes,
a lace curtain sways in an open window.

Children watch the lace sway, out and back.
They listen to birds sing like water in dark trees. They sing back.

I listen to the children. They are making the world up.
They are learning it by heart.

On the water it is cool.
The sun is small there and drifts with the wind.

It is very old. It comes from very near
and very far away.

The Ghost of the Ancestor Wakes

The farther I ride, bareback, drinking mares' milk,
the farther the horizon recedes before me,

the faster it closes in behind, sweeping me on.
The light trembles on the bearded lips of the iris.

In the cool wind of night water, as I walk
out among the trembling moon and stars,

a char butts against my legs, cold.
The moon is the heart behind clouds.

It is the first breath of storm in the evening,
when a body leaps up and the leaves sing,

green birds that have broken out of their cages
as farmers prod their god with pitchforks and he gets up and moves on.

Preliminary Notes to a Translation
of Particle Physics Into Platonic Light

When the stone falls into the hand
the hand closes on it in impatience.

The moon is a grain of wheat,
the sun a cockerel with a fiery tail, pecking in the gravel.

Then he goes to a wooden bucket full of water
and takes a cool drink.

That's where we come in, shaking hands all
the way around: hello, hello, hello, hello.

When the hand falls into the mind,
the mind closes on it in triumph.

That is to complete an act
and is necessary if we are to approach form

with less than a spray of dock seed for a staff.
When the mind falls into the body,

the earth closes on it in jubilation,
and darkness speaks.

Starlight, Starbright

A bird sits on the house and broods.
We are the people who have found ourselves on a knife ridge.

To the right the mountain falls into a valley of stone;
to the left it drops into the bed of a glacier.

We don't descend to the pastures anymore;
we don't trail behind deer slowly with a scythe.

We construct houses of snow on the peaks.
We crawl into them under the stars.

During the day the sun roars in our blue faces.
Then we don't understand a thing: light talks without words.

Those are the people who don't want to go up
and no longer go down. We say, "The weeds hold rain up to the air."

The cows search out violet shadows
under fir trees and stand there without moving

until the sun vanishes and the stars are here.
There is no point at which they are first seen.

The Harvest

Birds are perching on black twigs of bound fire.
The citizens are enraptured.

They stand on their rooftops,
they raise their arms to catch sparrows,

already they are singing; already
fledglings flare from their fingertips.

An iron night lies close over the earth all around.
Already the philosophers are speaking of pears,

the transubstantiation of matter
into the energy that vibrates within the rust of hearing.

They say it is the name of the night.
They say it is out of their control,

and they are laughing as they say it,
their ladders and climbing ropes over their shoulders,

their picking bags strapped to their chests,
even while the birds are flying south.

They stop. They listen. They are all
stopping and listening, even when they go on.

What the Birds Are Using Us For

In light the earth has projected the sun —
ancient birchbark codex of memory, fluttering.

Blackbirds trill of water from the brown birches: love poems, in sanskrit.
Yesterday I named ice. Now I name tomorrow's twigs.

The moon lies in a crescent along the shore. It trills.
The muskrat crouches in the ice drifts and washes his hands.

Yesterday, the eclipse. The last time we saw the sky is the first:
an old bone lying out among the reeds. A gathering.

The heron stares down through the heron for the bright fish
gone green as water that has gone still as sky. I stare back.

Certainty's Entrance Line

Poetry is dangerous as birds are dangerous.
Birds are dangerous to the concept of birds.

Plato wanted to be a poet, so set out to destroy poetry.
After three thousand years poetry and Plato are equally obsolete.

I can't bear certainty, but when I get up in the morning,
there it is, staring me straight in the face.

I spoke to my twin once: "If I step into the mirror I am the mountain."
It said: "If you want to be a mirror set out to destroy the mountain."

If men want to leave the state give them nothing from the state,
then see. If men sneer at words, give them a word

and watch them wince as they drop it,
but do not treat their hands for burns.

Who is the King Now?

The soldiers are still young. They have not yet
been given their weapons. Who's there?

The snails crawl up the garden wall and devour the roses.
At dawn they vanish very slowly:

late in the evening they are still there.
Young women stare through linen curtains.

They know nothing, except what their mothers have given away.
They know what is true. They know what is false.

At some point a monk must walk out the doors of the abbey
into the world, before the king's soldiers knock.

Song of the Earth

Men hesitate before the veils of eternity.
Only once do October flowers close their lips for the evening.

There is no bitterness in the world. It will soon be November.
The hand opens to the sound of the hand closing.

The hard questions of kingship are lost in the storm:
a baby born with a cowl. Look at this hair! It's as brittle as straw.

We live our one life behind a waterfall:
the film slowed down until the frames dance.

One yellow chrysanthemum with brown leaves
burns in the white world. Ah.

When I crush it between my fingers, it floods the air:
a dance, on flame. Ah, again.

Walking with the Black Bears
Along the September River

The blind dolphins of the Yangtze find their way like bats.
Only words strengthen the hardness of a stone.

In the end the quality of our tools is vital.
A world without water cannot quench or even wet a thirst.

The pear trees I planted in the garden are three feet tall:
I have been pulling weeds between this world and this word.

Waves crash and crash and crash on the edge of land.
Tide pools of light burn right within thought's perch. I climb around them.

After all these years, the stars arch and surge overhead:
the breath of the Big Bang as I walk beside the night river in shadow.

The earth is the sound of trees pulling up their roots and flying,
root to crown over the surface of the dark.

Death's Toast

A wave pours itself into water: breath through a flute.
From the hand in the mouth, the mouth in the thought.

In his dreams, the singer is a horse.
Only the grass knows where he runs: behind the mountains.

There is no mind. The people who have devoured the stars
sit in bars and laugh into the mounting dark.

If Death came now, I'd pour him a beer
and make a toast. What's love got to do with him?

He looks at me with sad eyes.
Who knows how sad? He clinks his glass.

Sunlight Over Timothy Hay Above Lac La Hache

This is the month of red-winged grasshoppers
with their wings like castanets: old lampshades.

They have learned to fly on red crinoline dresses.
As they clack and clatter, I lie back between the black-seeded clovers

with my eyes closed and the sun breathing my face.
The world is for an instant absolutely black,

an instant absolutely white,
then there are colours.

You read in old books that the world is illusion.
That is not it.

High Country Autumn

A black bird lifts its wings within the light.
A dog rises by sinking into the smoke of a potato field.

A woman in a red dress stands in a stone doorway
and swims into a blue sky. It will soon be night.

A wind out of the rushes howls in the meadows.
Daisies burning memory rust my differential. I mind.

A bell tolls in a ruined church by the river: fish scales.
It undulates close to the dead. Brown air.

After a dog's footsteps fill with cold water and colder sky,
leaves gather on the aspens, then fly.

One week ago, the moon was the mouth of a trout.
Now its green and pink fins fan above black hills.

Geese are gathering in shallow pans pock-marked with rain.
A woman is writing of angels in a book of water.

The crows have swallowed the sun. There is no earth.
Men dressed to confuse moose fill their engines with Regular Unleaded.

Day and night: beetles are covering the corpses of mice
where the owls dropped them on the path by the lake.

The hunting cats are staring down the toads in the dark.
In defense, the toads remain absolutely still.

The Eclipse of the Moon Viewed
Over the Cariboo Plateau

Birds walk low to the ground among the stalks of the wheat.
They are not afraid. It is late summer. No-one is afraid.

In their dreams the men and women stand in the night
on the peaks of their houses with their children between them

and stare up into the cold clear current where the earth
eats the moon. A pale wind combs their hair.

At the edge where it touches the hills with its hands
and breath and yellow feet the sky is never dark.

Now I realize how far we are from eternity.
We step slowly through it.

A loon rises before the beginning of the world.
The wind blows furiously yet the trees do not catch it at all.

It is good that the grass splashes with rain: the key of a piano
pressed lightly down into shadow and springing back.

I have dressed in my old coat of grass. I am fire.
I am fire. I have dressed in my old coat of grass.

In the Birdsong of a Bavarian Summer

All day, people step into the darkness of the mountains.
They wear canvas shoes with soles as thin as gloves.

The people walk out one at a time into the light,
then stand for a moment, still. They are absolute.

Until the young women run forward and slip their feet
into slow, green water, breath holds them. Then ice.

The river is the stars, pulling at the earth that God spoke.
Deer tripped out of fir saplings. Then they stopped.

They watched God with their big moon-eyes.
He kept on digging red clay from the stream bed shoes watch now.

When God blew his spirit into clay, a sparrow invented writing.
It was hard work. It turned God's lips blue.

Even today God is blowing with all his strength into the mud.
The deer have wandered off. Here we are now.

Angels are singing for the children in the meadows.
The notes fall onto the earth as rain. Creation has its pleasures.

Quarter notes flash through in the streambeds into the valleys, so loud
that when men speak to women, the women hear rushing water.

They lower their eyes to the clouds, that flow past their feet,
and sense how far they have come, and go on.

Mozart's Violin

The violin maker drinks fog through the window.
Calloused fingers tremble on the cold blue steel he draws.

Around his feet winged ants are running. Train cars climb the table.
Their bodies are filled with brandy four hundred years old.

It is the middle of the forest. The fog smells of stone and the skin
of a woman who stands in the light behind the light and dresses in straw.

A wolf has eaten the moon. He has devoured the sun and gnawed stars.
We are hunting an appetite in the hawthorn thickets under the railway bridge.

Sometimes the train roars by, delivering an avalanche,
and the earth heaves. Someday it is going to shake us all off.

The violins hang on the washing lines all summer, among sheets
that are soon taken down. We ripen in the sun, then we air.

Menhirs, Lac Neuchatel

Men come, on the far side of the door of the evening.
They leave it open a crack.

The sun is an ant crawling across a stone.
Emptiness is not a map, a road or a mill pond.

If you sense in the absolute darkness a fish
walking beside you, the darkness is not absolute.

Among yew trees, the blind reach out to touch the moon's scales.
The moon is a lake in November, beaten by coots.

If a char touches your skin with her fingers, leaf.
You are stone, with tall antlers and human hands.

A yellow wind rages out of the western hills.
We come back from death with a handful of thistle seeds.

An ant carries the last human words into the mouth of her nest.
We catch.

The Irises Given to Me by a Man Who
Once Grew Apples for Stalin

The irises flood the room with the scent of pebbles
filtering moonlight along the platinum river.

The state of the Big Bang in the long morning after:
dandelions littering the lawn's leaf litter,

their veins filled with a white and bitter milk —
the stars among us. At last, it is November.

In some months, men wish their houses were built of stones
grubbed up from the fields and set in place by hand,

where they can live with children
and know nothing but the world. I rack my wine.

Summer follows gravity into sterile glass, but the words
wish they were stones that could be picked up by the hands and thrown.

At 5 pm, the flowers burn us away as they sit beside the bed, living.
We get up in the dark and stare at them in the dark,

the house like small scraps of prayer
set loose on the flood-water, leaving us.

Green Man Rises

Women and the men walk grey fields together, their brightly-coloured
anoraks pulled tightly against the drumming wind.

Around them flames rise out of the glacial soil: clay
dolls hardened in fire and breathed full. I knock the top off mine.

People are amphorae: swollen, wide-hipped,
formed by hand and with the understanding of the hands;

filled by the mouth and with the understanding of the mouth
and what it can say, and what it cannot.

The earth has a different signature in every season:
when the dawn flares, the light lifts out of the coarse

grey fabric of the air itself and the canvas of a man's
fingers flutters as it catches that wind,

almost tugs off the bone of light that hold it within,
and someone stretches a green hand out of the soil, into the sky.

At the End of the World the World Is Born

Existence is a dimension of disintegration
but then so is a snail a dimension of a stone.

The gloves are carving hands out of agate
as playthings for their children.

The Sound of a River Breathing
in the Boat of Your Ribs

The river sniffs his way down among prickly pear and mock orange.
The books are dreaming the children, spines and all.

Night wears an amulet made of fired clay painted blue,
with one eye made of an apple seed and its mouth stuffed with salt.

Fish swim out of our tongues into the house of the sun,
each with a lump of fire in its throat, caught,

trembling, between the two halves of the world.
It is as if a vast storm has stilled on the shores of a grey, northern sea;

the trees on the rock outcrops stand for a moment, tall,
so soaked with rain that even one drop more would dissolve.

As the moon enters the eye of a trout rising to the surface of the sky,
the sun rises in the other eye and opens it.

Rereading an Old Book of Poems
on Leaving the High Plateau

The firs in the savannas talk secwepemctsin.
In old fenceposts, midnight country and western music still sings, faintly.

Robert Graves wrote that the White Goddess has three faces.
In his time, Lorca's poetry became a German tax dodge.

I write that the moon has the face of a Hereford cow
eating dandelions amongst the milkweed. I'm not bitter.

Grass gives voice to the wind blowing through the rangeland.
A stream threads light passing through stones boys turn over.

In the gaps between words sandhill cranes travel north, then south.
Here, they nest.

One day, a stone turner's daughters are learning to dance the five positions.
To see into the mind, look into the farthest distance.

I speak the old language of the frogs: water in drought.
The crusades are back. I remember flowers: fire in stone.

A flock of starlings swims in the deep of the lake,
wheeling in the last green shadows of the sun. Then water.

Then water. Then water.
Then water. Then water.

Ripples on the Pool of the Night
above Similkameen Station

The sun is a million points of flame in the seedheads.
The moon is a blue stone in the shadows.

I found it only today, in a white rain mixed with hail.
There are no words for the sky, so I say the other ones.

The flicker hammers at the cabin wall every morning at 5:20,
and continues even when I open the door

and step out into the solid yellow light and gasp.
The world is close.

Within the mind, the cabin
resounds like a wooden bell, struck with a tongue of grass.

Poem for the Woman of Apolda, Who Was Unloading Groceries From a Taxi While the Driver Smoked a Cigarette

In May, I walked into a church made of roses.
It had a leaking roof and a pastor who looked to the floor.

In November, I found the remains of a fishing boat on the sand,
and golf balls. I live in the shadow of clouds.

I know a musician who cannot read music.
He started off stealing cars; now he owns cars people have discarded.

When I was a boy, we celebrated Christmas by playing cards.
Now we celebrate the preparations for it.

Anaxagoras said appearances are a glimpse of the unseen.
He also said the descent to Hades is the same, no matter where you start.

Now that our children have found each other, where
do we find our children if not in ourselves?

Skelton said a wall without pictures is a house with no windows.
Anaxagoras said everything has a natural explanation.

When I went to university, I signed up to study philosophy.
They tried to teach me obedience. I kept one hand behind my back.

Across from the church of Maria in Apolda is a statue
of what a man feels when he looks at a woman. Oh, those communists.

When I returned from the East, I said I had lost all my pictures.
No. I had found them.

A Remedy for Any Man Unable to See
the Forest for the Trees

Antisthenes said that not to unlearn what you have learned
is the most necessary kind of learning. He died in 371 BC.

At some other time he said that the most useful piece of learning
for the uses of life is to unlearn what is untrue. Then again, there are ravens.

Antisthenes was born in 444. BC. The ravens of Prince Rupert
have made a language out of anchors clanging against fog.

The ravens of Vancouver Island have constructed a language out
of old growth cedars rubbing against wind. It has outlasted the trees:

for three hundred miles, not one original tree has been left standing.
In the fall, people gather huckleberries from the stumps. Ah, wilderness.

Among a colonial people, poetry is synonymous with self-expression.
Even Antisthenes knew that — not that it helped.

Before we knew better, we said the sun rose in the morning.
Now that we turn towards it, we still do.

I Begin My New Life as a Thermometer Now

When the poet left the mountains, he brought his Egyptian onions.
Then he lost them. After a year and a half, one has come back to life.

I saw Jesus rise from the cobblestones in Recklinghausen.
Just north of town there is a private preserve for wild horses.

The storm building now is predicted to crest at midnight.
I have learned to believe in miracles as miracles.

I used to believe a stone was a matrix of energy, with no weight.
Nothing I have learned in the last thirty years contradicts that.

Diogenes said most men are within a finger's breadth of being mad.
Don't stand under winter roofs when the weather is turning.

Out in the strait, fishermen are shooting sea lions.
The pride of a people is drifting with the sea change and the buoy's bell.

An old man plants cabbages to make sauerkraut for a village
that has become a series of photographs. He trained with the blacksmith.

Diogenes said it takes a wise man to discover a wise man.
Sometimes it takes a fool.

Diogenes said a lot about the sun. The poet warms his fingers.
He drinks water from a mountain, but first he brings it up to room
temperature.

Storm on the Island Shore

Diogenes said the foundation of every state is the education of its youth.
Without that, there are leeks, there is parsley and there are lettuces.

The wind is buffeting the house. I am reminded of poppies.
A civilization can be built up out of a seed catalogue.

If I think of each word as a card on a prayer wheel,
I also think of the way the words that come to my lips come to life.

For miles, people sit in their cars and watch the ocean reach for them,
knowing full well that it does no such thing.

Certainty is not certainty. Terror is not joy. Not exactly.
Change alone is unchanging, said Heraclitus. Not exactly.

Under deep snow, the ground remains unfrozen.
In an age of advertisement, an ocean is not a bladderwrack.

In an age of promotion, a man's character is not his fate.
Out of us, Heraclitus would have made a destiny.

On the one hand, thing rhymes with thing.
On the other hand, I hold you when the lights go out.

After thirty years, Adam and Eve had named all the weeds.
After thirty years, I am still planting new gardens.

All along the coast, branches snap from the trees. Every bladderwrack
tossed up on the beach contains mouthfuls of the sky coming home.

How to Be From Somewhere in Particular

Luther's father was a coal miner.
He went down to Hell and brought up heat.

There's no point in waxing nostalgic.
The spirit of all philosophers is as bodiless in life as in death.

When Luther was hiding from the Pope, he dressed as a knight.
This is the same story as the one in which he was kidnapped.

He lived in the same castle in which a woman turned bread into roses.
She fed the poor with that. They were much nourished.

The troubadours of those forests composed poems about birds.
Birds don't compose poems. They recombine notes.

A rose that puts out flowers also puts out thorns.
This was once considered miraculous. Then not. Then it is again.

The oldest roads follow the deepest valleys.
The men on the hilltops were not traveling.

They were probably brigands. Come, to be
at home in the world, be the road. Go.

What the Pharoahs Would Say of
Our Country Between Worlds

Some windows are made of glass and some of screens
to shut out insects. Some men are opened that way too.

An icon is not a window into heaven.
We are that. We ascend by concrete staircases.

There is no art to the creation of icons.
They create artless men. Infinity did not invent zero.

In museums, too much light surrounds the saints.
The space around them is blind, but not exactly ash.

Icons are created from fifty layers of wax and lacquer.
Hand-broken pieces of stone work just as well.

The painters of the Renaissance realized they could dabble on wet plaster.
Ever since then, beauty has been skin deep.

Admirable men used to be crowned with gold.
Unfortunately, they crowned kings.

If you pull back a curtain you do not find Heaven.
You find a window.

In Birnau, the angels have discovered a beehive.
They dip their fingers into it, and lick. Such infants!

Wearing a Dead Man's Suit

Where does the sea end: at the waves, at the shingle,
at the cedars, at the peaks, at the grasslands, never, ever?

Only the crests of the waves are visible in the dark.
At one time, this was a matter for touch and hearing.

The Eiffel tower was commissioned to hold a spotlight
that would turn night into day. Now do you understand economics?

If a movie could be filmed in the dark and viewed in darkness
it would be the body. We leave all retakes for our children.

On a dark and stormy night, I was supposed to be writing a novel.
Instead, I reassembled the skeletons in my closet until they hung me.

If I were a suit, I would say, "Put me on. Wear me." But I am
a dead man's suit. I say, "You're putting me on." Aren't you?

For Joanne, Who Says that Venus is the Goddess of Poetry

The knife knows a kind of rain that reminds thought of metal.
Romanticists expect their children to court each other in science class.

For emotional guidance, they give the kids each other.
A blue heron takes flight by tiptoeing on its hands. I try it. Oh my.

My friend Ken paints with neon and industrial processes,
while the poets are asking if there is a wilderness.

Some words are misleading, like 'goddess'.
As the waves crash at my feet I eat an apple from a cold hand.

Every age of the world has its own signature,
but I wouldn't tell the deer that, out in the forest.

I knew a silver river and bursting milkweed.
Who are you going to tell about something like that now?

Struck by Lightning

I used to climb the highest limbs of the walnut. I stopped
because old men took the nuts away, unhulled.

There is a kind of rain that reminds my body of wood,
a slow and imperceptible flame shedding its water.

Dogs walk barefoot, everywhere. Poets are shaking political
cages while living out the last days of the earth.

What follows the garden is a desert.
What follows a desert is not the Garden.

I have a friend who photographs angels with broken noses.
It's not stone that makes a mountain.

Artists who are the engineers of new technologies
know more about forklifts than warehouses.

It is said that Robin Hood darkened his skin with the hulls of walnuts.
You now do that with an artificial sun, at your stylist's.

I come from a people who once worshipped trees
as frozen bolts of lightning. They became the salt of the earth.

A Pilgrim's Song on the Road to the East

God is at home. It's we who have gone out for a walk,
says Meister Eckhart. All pilgrimages are linear.

Some roads lead through forests.
Some lead into them. Some are thickets.

I came upon a deer giving birth under ancient trees.
It took a long time before I saw her tremble.

Sometimes a living man is shorter than the grass.
This is different than saying that dead ones are.

By the sea, a man feels the rain on his face without lifting it.
When all the trees die, the grass returns.

Only the hand that erases can write the true thing,
says Meister Eckhart. Some men think it's about the erasing.

I went to Germany looking for minstrels.
Who needs a minstrel when one is traveling? asks the devil.

I discovered a country where church steeples wear helmets.
Or was it a country in which soldiers wore church steeples?

I have felt the dead blow through the grass while young men
laughed with young women. They share this with each other.

I have mud on my shoes.
This is how I enter the cathedral: on foot.

The Niceties of Foreshore Ownership

First the storm, then the raccoon knocking on the front door.
The dog sleeping late on the steps curls around his snout.

In Germany, waiters are the new upper class
of a society that knows how to patent moss. They teach impatience.

In Canada, doorhandles are brass bedposts tipped with skulls.
And the French said of the Germans, you are so German! So French.

At the high tide line, shrimp are piled ankle deep.
I squeak along the bay in my runners, too committed to turn back.

People are hurling driftwood out of their musk roses
to a tide that will toss it back next November. They wear gumboots.

For the most part, crows ignore us.
At other times, they die laughing.

The Parade Square Napoleon Made of Erfurt

A man sits in a waiting room. When he boards a train,
it takes him to another waiting room. Rooms make time.

The last temperate grassland is in British Columbia, which governs
by selling licenses for coal bed methane. Governs whom? What?

The ferries are closed down on the Fraser River, because of ice.
Replaced by libraries, writers choose to write about memory.

A group of transsexual women in Ohio worship Cybele.
In the universities, Plato still hasn't been given his hemlock.

If the Church is the body of God, why are there tourists?
If Plato were given hemlock this afternoon, would he drink it?

Lucas Cranach the Elder made Mary, Mother of God, achingly beautiful.
It took hours for his model to crimp her red hair into ringlets.

In an age in which a woman was asked to model the art of waiting,
men were their own judges and their own executioners.

We may have forgotten the dead in the Polish struggle for freedom.
They have certainly forgotten us.

Haunting Ghosts

John Dee wrote down the language of angels.
Then he burnt it. Then he wrote it down again.

Queen Elizabeth rode through the geese on holiday.
In this way, she spread plague throughout England.

After a storm, old men pick up branches from the grass.
You can find them by thin plumes of blue smoke in the trees.

An old woman who drinks too much in the afternoons
reads mystery novels. This is the new inquisition.

Jesuits know how to argue a point. My hairdresser neither argues
nor expects her answers to conform to reason. She pitches softball.

The local custom is to park the boat in the garage and the car on the street.
All novelists are students of architecture.

Church steeples have bells to call the faithful to prayer.
In truth, they were built as fire lookouts and pigeon coops.

Where the storks have returned in Germany, they are fed with chickens.
Beauty is not necessarily about dignity or wilderness.

French women who loved Germans were shaved bald and then hung.
They are still not the ones who appear ugly.

40,000 men shipped out on U-boots in the Atlantic. 10,000
found their way home again. They were all haunted. I am too.

The Green Imagination in the Time
of Chickadees and Amaranth

In storm, the rain becomes a field of wheatgrass, in 4-D.
At the opening of Witness God delivers fields of bread.

Before the murders, every mystery is two people doing lunch.
It's easy to forget that Lear is just a stone mask eroding.

The secret of writing a play is to play. The clue
to writing a novel is to be novel. This doesn't help with cricket.

Some saints are honoured for their miracles, others
for being killed. All are political. None are voters. None did.

I know a woman who says we shouldn't teach, except ourselves.
She will argue it until late in the night, then she will serve eggs.

I used to graft apple trees, then steal grapes from ruined vineyards.
The Green Man has shaved his beard and cranked down the heat.

Memory is a drug. It sorts illusions from the moments
that created them. Some call this love.

On its way to the sea, the rain pours into the gutter
with the sound of tiny bells. I could listen to it all night.

The Day We Reenacted the Story of the Trinity

Eisenach

Each walnut splits in two halves, like a brain.
Like the brain, they are held together by the tongue.

Our cities used to serve our farmers.
Now our farmers serve them.

Up the coast, wolves swim five miles between islands.
Tonight, they are my name as the moon glows in the surf.

Communist children used to play with lead Indians.
Their parents also manufactured soldiers and cowboys.

I met a retired farmer who lives on $128 a month.
Writers don't retire. They rest on the lip of each paragraph.

While grocers were selling produce in the market,
a beggar was giving himself away in a twenty-year-old shirt.

Politics is often a matter of punctuation: exclamations,
quotes, commas, semi-colons, colons and periods.

Forbidden to feed the poor, St. Elizabeth became poor herself.
She died of starvation.

Bach stands in the doorway of a church shaped like a woman,
but we are the ones who push the inner door open.

Every woman was once a virgin and every man a holy spirit.
Then it's Christmas and the organ fills all the space there is.

The Grammar of the Road

In a ruined city, I can hold the sky with my hands.
On the road, I reach up yet cannot, among trees that can.

In bloom, the apple trees look like birds planted on the hillsides.
For a hundred miles, every hawthorn is trying to fly in space.

I want to stop the car and call out, ***Look everyone, dance!***
On roads like this, there is no space outside of cities.

Post-unification agriculture: every roadside stand sells asparagus.
It is grown in none of these fields. They grow daisies.

Theophrastus said superstition is cowardice in the face of the supernatural.
I was a child raised by trees. I thought each snowflake was a fallen star.

If it has not snowed enough, it will. The army spends the day
setting up to play music for the people: well, chairs.

The local palace is called the Castle of Peace.
It was built at the end of a war, not at its beginning.

In the gnostic tradition, God is an imposter.
The real God is the world. He is chips of light on the water.

In the tradition of deserts, trees are mirages.
Still, they give shade, and dates.

Kings once planted trees, so their grandsons could build ships.
Many of those trees are now old and losing their branches to trucks.

In the existential tradition, there are grammars but no answers.
We are waiting for our selves to reveal themselves to us.

Between the Crabapples and the Grass

I lived with clowns once. I dressed in sadness
and stretched it to fit my mouth. It tore at the corners.

When crows dress in diamonds, I will bring the coal out of my closet
that I wore at my wedding. Apricots carry their heat into the night.

A black dog at midnight is the approach of darkness.
To feel the rain is not the same as mapping the river.

Sacred groves were often marked by sheepskins
shorn from the sun. The sun is now a self-contained explosion.

When a people are driven from their homeland,
weeds grow in graveyards. They bring their dead with them.

The secret of selling asparagus is to soak it in water.
What is free is often the most dear.

It is when a people abandons their dead
that they begin to replace them with the living.

It is not true that an angel can dance on the head of a pin.
Neither is it false. When a clown opens its mouth, it has teeth.

Every day the blackbirds return to the sunflowers.
Every day the sunflowers bend closer to the earth.

The Philosophy of Weaving

The sensation of texture, drawn over, makes a line human.
Its viewer sees a mirror of a mirror of a mirror of an error.

Nietzsche never said what he was thinking, yet people knew.
His readers were the ghost that walked, always, in his shadow.

A graffiti artist lives to write his name on a train,
yet his travels are blind and take place without him.

Many men are working, consciously, to dismantle civilization.
Everyday life is beginning to approach the condition of music.

To ban artists has always been the strong man's temptation.
When he realizes he is one, he bans critics and lemons.

To shoot meditators from Britain is not an act of war.
To be shot while meditating is not an act of découpage.

The writers are arguing: shall they join Hamas? Shall they weep?
This would never have happened while they still wrote on paper.

Words printed on paper once had a sense of duration.
At the universities, they are now retrieved by electric robots.

What is the difference between an asparagus field and a museum?
It is the never-narrowing gap between a child and its children.

A Life Among the Ghosts of Celtic Winemakers

After he wrote his epic, Rilke wrote about trench bombardment
and the resulting deafness. Tragically, even Rilke has become an angel.

That part of me that lives in a medieval tapestry
flutters its wings and sings above the hunters.

As my own reader, alive in a woven forest,
I am beginning to unclip the dogs from their leashes.

My grandmother said, "No child ever caught a pigeon."
There are some things that pass all understanding.

After a certain age, every man is his own father.
After a certain age, every man is his own father's father.

Either I have been followed by spies, or I have travelled
to their favourite places: elevators and bakeries.

A man trained as an engraver for princes makes school books
for children. This was called an economic miracle, once.

View From the North Star's Gallery of Mirrors

A grain of wheat is not an economic revitalization.
Swallows gather mud beneath a dripping tap and fly with it.

An almond is a peach without juice or sweetness.
Painters are hypnotists; only the mad wear straight jackets.

The art of counting begins without art.
Even a bishop is an artwork made out of biology.

Life is not a theory. Neither are systems.
Not every doubter doubts his doubt, or believes his certainty.

Some communities are not beside the road but on it.
It is men in orange jumpsuits who erect maypoles.

In the oldest cities, children are paid to have children.
Politics is sometimes a matter of stating the obvious.

Late at night, I look north into darkness.
I have the same view when I look south.

Men do not reveal themselves by what they see,
but what they see reveals them.

Libretto for a Field of Daisies

Music is a field of silence. The notes are stones.
In the Welsh mountains, every wall is its own gate.

A leaf is built out of soil and sun. So are bricks. Only a man
who does not know work looks on art as an act of contemplation.

There is more engineering in a chair than in a house.
To see into peasant kitchens, the inquisitors merely lifted up their roofs.

A man who sits has more dignity than one who stands,
if the chair is raised on a dais. This does not apply to milk stools.

The Olympics were founded as a way to train for war.
Do you expect me to believe they are now a way to train for peace?

Never end with a question unless you know the answer:
unless you mean to begin right here.

At the End of the Earth, Begin Swimming

During a rainfall, the world is emptied of discussions
about the origin of God. There are pearls on the forest ferns.

So much of what men write is only the recognition
that the world is their selves. Truth bears repeating.

The invisible masterpiece is not the mountain
behind the chains of rain. It is not a goat's footfall.

A friend starts the new year by asking if Dionysus is dangerous.
It is never safe to write a poem in a mirror.

People once carried their houses on their backs.
Then they set them down at the roadsides for the mercy of strangers.

In our selves, we are as naked as Adam and Eve,
but not as naked as cormorants between rains.

On a windy coast, there is no point to umbrellas.
Their creators are shy deer hidden in a forest of outstretched hands.

If you fall and someone offers you her hand, give her yours.
If she falls, fall faster.

The Water Circus

The bodies of men are thin seed pods in Autumn's cold nights.
The sun holds absolutely still. It is an old language.

In a system of relations abandoned by men for the drugs of words,
men worship blindness, not justice.

Artists paint intricate tombs with the beginning of the world.
It is best to keep walking through the flames of books.

It is not a human world. The wind soughs in the trees
as the trees sough in the wind. Words, words, words.

The sun falls to earth as the earth falls into the sun.
A man at dawn walking through a field of grass

wet with dew is a field of grass walking into a man.
In the dew, the sun hangs in its entirety

off each finely-carved grass blade.
A conflagration of stars. A barbiturate. Speed.

Where Time Ends and Eternity Begins

Nietzsche said what determines your rank
is the quantum of power you are: the rest is cowardice.

Clear cut forests recede into blue hills
in sheets of smoke, which they enter as they reenter light.

A deer steps out of trees, over rocks white with lichen
fed on summer's spray: a waterfall in a heart's fire.

Snow clouds outlined in white drift down from the north.
A green band of light hovers over the horizon: a spirit level.

Birds may flit above the glare of the lake,
but the trout swim, dulled with cold, within the hands.

I wrote once that hands formed as an earth rich with rivers
and held the soil up to the star road. The dead walk.

Tonight, the ocean has turned to breath, with stars.
Ah language, now you have us.

Water's Song Is of Two Minds

Every kokanee plunges into deep cold with an aha.
Priests in purple gowns carry willows through the crypts.

In the stream a kokanee does not see the stream.
It is the windows of Edinburgh that swirl overhead.

Built by hand out of wax, we are burning
the silver off of the far side of a mirror.

For twenty years, I was a pear tree above the lake.
Evening is a flower, folded out of crêpe paper and white wine.

The wave came before the willow, but not to me.
Between snows in April, black branches bloom with ivory flowers.

In long evenings after cool rain, Aeneas returns to Troy.
In darkness, each bud is a page from the Talmud.

Each leaf is the moment after a match is extinguished, or before it is lit.
Pears are a memory of snow, yet they both fall.

In storm, the lake is a black amphora, with its white horses.
A bull snake first spoke the word 'grass'. I whisper it back.

The sun that drenches the grass halms ends right there,
where we begin. Where we end. Where we begin again.

An Admonition to Drink Your Coffee While it Is Hot

In the electric grate, Athena dusts Odysseus's hair with gold.
After a long journey, men approach a door, bearing an empty cup.

The sagebrush burns in a hundred saffron torches.
The first lie: the trees are not the wind. I rattle my fingers.

On his deathbed, Baudelaire revised the critique of pure reason.
A crow flies through the passage of its absence.

When the world collapses into the past, men are matches.
There was a time when they were given away free, as advertisements.

If you find a ruffed grouse nesting in an ashtray, strike.
If you find only ashes, it was not a grouse, or you were, only a moment ago.

Walking Out of the Cave Is
Not the Same as Wisdom

Men call to the faces of days that have long left them.
The white flashes of leaves turn over in wind.

The sky is calling for snow, and nothing is quickening.
The sunlight pours through the strings of the moon's piano.

Blackbirds flare up over the house into the mouth of the sun.
What we teach our children, still: words, words, words.

Each grain cast to chickens is a sentence lost from language.
This life has no duration.

A journey never begun, never ended: never ended, never begun.
When in doubt, doubt when.

Each of the thousand leaves of an aspen sapling
turns the same way to face the sun, then releases it.

The choice is not to discard the greasepaint, but to walk back
to a shutter of sparrows.

Each eye burns for an instant, then goes dark,
then darker. Then there are stars.

Trees Drink the Ocean that Drinks the Trees

Birds scatter up, black against the sun.
As they recede into the hills, darkness gloves all men.

The burden of memory becomes elaborate over time:
as a child, I had a cricket in my ear. I stepped outside to catch it.

The first grammar and the last: men do not fly off
with the blackbirds above marsh cinquefoil. Their presence does.

Song, song, song, song, song, song: a happy drunkenness. Song.
Snow dropping into still water floats among trout, then dissolves.

The elm and its leaves, the body and the hand,
breathe. I will not not mention love.

The dancer and the mask, the carved mouth and the voice:
the stone knife in the arm. Each muscle was once a clam.

The dancers breathe the tree the mask was carved from. It is passing.
We are on a journey towards the here and now, now and here.

Giving Oneself to the Path

Land is the thought of a hawk hunting.
Wise men are paid for fiddly work with silence.

The cathedral is an exquisitely calibrated machine for drowning.
What the night knows vanishes when the sun

climbs on its feathered legs over the distant edge of its desert.
I have learned a new lingo, but with whom can I trade it?

Deer step out of deep grass one word at a time,
and step into it at the same pace: pilgrims.

The fire at the end of the twig: the twig at the tip of the hand.
A bear stands in my shape, facing the driving snow.

What we can know is what we can never say.
I cast the words I speak into the night; they return as the world.

I open the door to stare at myself opening it.
Some days it is enough that there is still a door.

A Man and His Doppelgänger Speak as One

Every night I open the box of the snow among black trees.
In this way I keep alive the message men give to the earth.

There is a body that stands within this body, that moves when it moves.
In the bite of a cold wind, I remember the moment of birth.

The sun fills the hollow space in each stalk of grass.
If it wasn't for death, the streets would be full of corpses.

We have been here for years, watching armies pass in the night.
The old saying is not true: all roads do not lead to Rome.

When we forget ourselves, we speak as grass.
When we remember, the grass speaks us.

The Hidden Ones Reveal Themselves

The human night is soundless and indestructible.
Even in the dark, lovers cry out.

The last of the guttural languages is still spoken among the trees.
The taste of apples is within the star of their seeds.

Within a block of cedar: a stillness the carver seeks not to touch.
The wind plays the breves and reedy rests of the sparrows.

On a shore, the earth is only the sound of breakers.
Old words come to mind, and stay there.

Everywhere, the body cries out.
The mind, in hiding, doesn't.

A Conversation in Starlight With a Child With Grey Hair

The children say the philosophers have returned.
It is possible only to grasp certainties: the weight of an apple.

One day the leaves suddenly burst out of the twigs of the poplars.
I push out of breath against a heavy torrent.

The sun replaces the notes of the body at the same rate they sweep away into the dark.
The man you were yesterday has already flowed away, and now the man you are.

My breath forms birds before me in the air.
In spring, after months of snow, my breath returns, singing.

In the kingdom of memory, there are no messages.
The thundering of horses on the packed sand of the shore vanishes into the surf.

I swim through the man who stays. Bees
circle his head and lay honey in his lungs. Then it rains.

The Merciful Shade of Trees
Against the Merciless Sky

In summer, horses are lead into the forests to fill their eyes with water.
On holiday, the king is just a country a month away from the city.

Only philosophers are permitted to keep birds.
Pigeons wheel in mathematical curves, apart but never separate.

Words once lived and walked amongst men, dressed as they dressed.
A hyena growls in the clink of a teacup.

War drives young lovers into green grass.
To men of softer ethics, the needs of empire are paramount.

Dangerous are the ten thousand footsteps that draw a man from the river.
On the tundra, only stone men point the way to shelter.

In the highest towers, philosophers are imprisoned with their stars.
Mercifully, the glaring light of day obliterates the thought of this.

The breath indrawn during love making: the lift of a horse's head.
The dying invent for themselves a meaning for memory and identity.

There are trees of coal below the cliffs where the swallows nest.
I carry mud one mouthful at a time from the falls to the sky.

Memory is blue. There is a moon in it.
I climb to it on a ladder of sound,

then on the sound of a ladder, then on breath,
then I stop climbing.

The Word That Changes the World

The walls of our houses have the insubstantiality of night wind.
The walls of the wind's house has ours.

The business of philosophers is the murder of children.
The play of children is the murder of philosophers.

Odysseus built his house around a tree: a torch for his voyage.
The bassoonist blows one note over and over. And over. And over.

The caress of grass blades against bare legs: March rain beading on windows.
At dusk, people shiver: they have no shadows — or they all have one.

History: to steal another man's wife, court a forest
that marched across the hills to your walls and said your name out loud.

Messengers From a World Before Marx's Ascension

Clouds float on the edge of the sky,
on which are painted chubby little boys trailing ribbons and flowers.

Children play unaware of the price to be paid
when one has heard the world without artifice.

How old is the earth? Ships cross the spice routes,
laden with plastic backscratchers made in Shanghai.

When God made the world, he covered it with green industrial linoleum.
Birds move unseen in the treetops, but it is better to speak the things of the world:

the small tree frogs come out in the rain;
young men read about the hierarchies of angels.

The lost political economy is the passion for starlight,
the folding of the left hand over the right.

Noon is a reed that men might learn to walk from,
or so they believe. Pity them. Believe in them;

it grows uncomfortably cold at midsummer.
Dogs are barking like stars from every street corner.

When the whole city vanishes into the sound of rain,
you are the price of the world. Otherwise, the debt.

A man appears at the door of a valley of wind,
with two bottles of wine and a mouth without teeth.

There is a love that surpasses knowledge,
but has the same name. You have just answered to it.

The Creation of the World Starts Now

Begin with something of which you can be certain:
never end with a statement asking to be filled.

After the silence of the night tiny birds speak in the meadows
I spill coffee. I make more before cleaning the kitchen.

The black book, which contains the secret history of the city,
was lost in a war. All wars are lost and found in peace.

Publicly speaking, after the cleaning of bricks, men and women
chose to rebuild the earth for themselves, in private.

No-one needs to speak the word that one becomes.
Work cannot speak what it is not, but men labour at it.

A green crown of trees sways on the horizon.
I came out without a shirt. I shiver, in leaves.

I read that God made the earth out of darkness and water.
No, he is making it as we speak.

The Snow of the Universe

When lovers become strangers,
there is no longer a sky. There is a black tree.

The crow struts from branch to branch
much more slowly than rain.

The bear moves through the hunter.
The hunter is as sharp as his breath, but no sharper.

One mote of light, then nothing
for twenty paces then one mote of light.

Acknowledgements

I would like to thank the British Columbia Arts Council for providing a grant for writing the oceanside poems in this book.